Clay and Star

Also by **Liliana Ursu** (translated into English):

The Sky Behind the Forest, translated by Liliana Ursu, Adam J. Sorkin, and Tess Gallagher (Bloodaxe Books, 1997)
Angel Riding a Beast, translated by Bruce Weigl and Liliana Ursu (Northwestern UP, 1998)
Goldsmith Market, translated by Sean Cotter (Zephyr Press, 2003)
Lightwall, translated by Sean Cotter (Zephyr Press, 2009)
A Path to the Sea, translated by Adam J. Sorkin, Liliana Ursu, and Tess Gallagher (Pleasure Boat Studio, 2011)

Also by **Mihaela Moscaliuc:**

EDITED COLLECTION:
Insane Devotions: On the Writing of Gerald Stern (Trinity University Press, 2016)

POETRY:
Immigrant Model (University of Pittsburgh Press, 2015)
Father Dirt (Alice James Books, 2010)

TRANSLATIONS:
The Hiss of the Viper by Carmelia Leonte (Carnegie Mellon University Press, 2014)
Death Searches for You a Second Time by Carmelia Leonte, co-translated with Michael Waters (Red Dragonfly Press, 2003)

Clay and Star

Selected Poems by **Liliana Ursu**
Translated by **Mihaela Moscaliuc**

etruscan press

Etruscan Press
Wilkes University
84 West South Street
Wilkes-Barre, PA 18766
(570) 408-4546

 Wilkes
University

www.etruscanpress.org

Published 2019 by Etruscan Press
Printed in the United States of America
Cover image: Last Judgment (1487) mural detail, Pătrăuți Monastery
Cover design by James Dissette
Interior design and typesetting by Julianne Popovec
The text of this book is set in Adobe Garamond.

First Edition

17 18 19 20 5 4 3 2 1

Library of Congress Cataloguing-in-Publication Data

Names: Ursu, Liliana, 1949- author. | Moscaliuc, Mihaela, 1972- translator.
Title: Clay and star : selected poems / by Liliana Maria Ursu ; translated by
    Mihaela Moscaliuc.
Description: First edition. | Wilkes-Barre, PA : Etruscan Press, 2019.
Identifiers: LCCN 2018017733 | ISBN 9780999753439
Subjects: LCSH: Ursu, Liliana, 1949---Translations into English.
Classification: LCC PC840.31.R82 A2 2019 | DDC 859/.134--dc23
LC record available at https://lccn.loc.gov/2018017733

Please turn to the back of this book for a list of the sustaining funders of Etruscan Press.

This book is printed on recycled, acid-free paper.

For Andrei and Alexandru

Clay and Star: Selected Poems

Acknowledgments

These translations would not be what they are without the exquisite editorial eye and musical ear of poet Michael Waters, early co-translator and constant supporter. Much gratitude goes to Liliana Ursu for her assistance and valuable editorial input, as well as to the editors of the following journals, in which these translations appeared, sometimes in slightly different versions:

Absinthe: "Poem Written on a Rainy Day about Garden Shears," "Poem with Blueberries, Fog, and Sibiu," "Prayer"
America: "The One Who Leaves Few Footprints in the Snow"
This Broken Shore: "Father Cleopa," "In the Heart of the Forest"
Connotation Press: An Online Artifact: "The Barn," "Messenger," "Stigmata"
Crazyhorse: "The Biblical Gardens of San Francisco," "The Child Speaks"
Hayden's Ferry Review: "Dusk with Poet"
The Marlboro Review: "Poem with Wax Wicket," "Spring Fire," "Poem in January," "Chimney Sweepers between Millennia"
Modern Poetry in Translation (U.K.): "The Tower of Steps," "Painting with Late Night in Păltiniș," "Harmonia Mundi," "The Main Square," "The Little Square," "The Bridge over the Train Station," "Between the Wheat Wells and the Bridal Mirrors"; "The Tower of Steps" and "Between the Wheat Wells and the Bridal Mirrors" were reprinted in *Modern Poetry in Translation: Centres of Cataclysm* (Bloodaxe, U.K., 2016)
New Letters: "Luggage," "The Light of the Psalms"
Poem (U.K.): "History of a Couple," "Landscape with Poet," "And Here Goes Tess, on Nygatan Street," "In the Burgh of Yesteryear," "Mother's Birth Year," "Sitting at the Table with My Angel in Patmos," "The Windows of Visby"; "History of a

Couple," "Landscape with Poet," "And Here Goes Tess, on Nygatan Street," and "In the Burgh of Yesteryear" were reprinted in *Bridge Eight*

Poetry International: "If I Lift my Eyes," "Poem with Wicket in Stephen the Great's Bell Tower"

Runes: "The Pine in the Bay"

Salamander: "Healings," "The Tower of Welders," "The Street of Measuring Scales"

The Stillwater Review: "Sibiu Rain" and "Poem with Stairway to the Hermit's Hut."

Clay and Star

Preface

In her native Romanian, Liliana Ursu has published thirteen collections of poems and two books of short fiction. For over a quarter century, she produced and presented an acclaimed weekly literary program for Romanian National Radio that focused on contemporary world poetry. Recipient of two Fulbright Fellowships to Penn State University and numerous prizes from the Romanian Writers' Union, Ursu was recently awarded Romania's highest cultural honor, the rank of Knight of Arts and Literature.

Ursu's first book in English, *The Sky Behind the Forest* (Bloodaxe Books, 1997), translated by Ursu, Adam J. Sorkin, and Tess Gallagher, was a British Poetry Book Society Recommended Translation and was shortlisted for Oxford's Weidenfeld Prize. Bruce Weigl facilitated Ursu's American debut with his translation of *Angel Riding a Beast* (Northwestern, 1998), and translator Sean Cotter further established her reputation as a major European poet with *Goldsmith Market* (Zephyr, 2003) and *Lightwall* (Zephyr, 2009), the latter a finalist for the PEN USA 2010 Literary Award in Translation. Ursu's most recent collection in English, *A Path to the Sea* (Pleasure Boat Studio, 2011), translated by Adam J. Sorkin and Tess Gallagher with the author, continued to build a readership and boost Ursu's reputation on the international scene.

Clay and Star comprises poems selected from Ursu's body of work. They capture the most distinguishing features of Ursu's voice while conversing with one another and deepening into or reframing certain obsessions. Ursu approaches the world with a divinely tuned ear, determined to rescue whatever beauty lies within, and with an eye keen on capturing with shimmering precision those spiritual and philosophical "nodes" where the sacred and the mundane converge. The poems of *Clay and Star* delineate an unabashed poetics of spirituality. Whether anchored in Sibiu (the poet's birthplace), Bucharest (Romania's capital), the magical monasteries of Bucovina, or in Greece, San Francisco, Louisville, or Lewisburg, they connect vast territories and cultures, establishing parallels and connections that elide differences or turn such differences into spaces of spiritual intimacy.

Ursu's work is highly esteemed by her fellow poets. Former U.S. Poet Laureate Mark Strand compared her poems to "flowers at the edge of the abyss. They are beautifully clear and precise, but behind them one glimpses the presence of an ineradicable dark." Slovenian poet Tomaž Šalamun called her "a dancer, an archeologist of light." "How she expands the places of myth," he adds, "is beyond grasping: your skin, your mind, your heart rejoice. Gracious, hard-edged, generous and moving." Tess Gallagher writes, "The silken web she weaves between continents, between her literature and ours, between her country's suffering under Ceausescu and abutting her experience of American abundance and freedom, has much to teach us. ... It is as if [through her work] we inhale some rare and deliciously saving perfume whose essence mysteriously extends our notion of what a soul is and what it requires when challenged to stand naked and humble before life's extremities."

Transporting Ursu's poems from one language and culture to another, much like the 'translating' of relics from one holy place to another, has been a humbling process. The stunning clarity of her poems may give the impression that they have slipped into English effortlessly. They did and they didn't. Her images are so chiseled and her diction so exacting in its demands for subtle music that the task was often daunting, though unfailingly rewarding.

Mihaela Moscaliuc

The Pine in the Bay

The air remains hot.
Confident,
I rest
in July's cage.
Like Daniel in the lions' den,
I survive in this town
slowly filling with linden trees and barbarians.

And I imagine solitude,
the unrelenting verticality
of the pine in the bay
and the sailors' battle with the sea
when Iona blessed their company:
that peaceful moment mid-storm
when they all abandoned their oars
to pray.

Poem Written on a Rainy Day about Garden Shears

On the table white as the sea wall
in de Chirico's painting
the poetry notebook and "Homilies on Repentance"
by St. John of the Cross.
Next to them the garden shears
with arms yellowish
like two candles,
the steel coil
unquestionable.

And last, the shears' blades
that trim all illusions,
all sins.
All the way to the bluish skin
caressed only by angels.

Poem with Wax Wicket

In each waxy hexagon
a word,
a grain of pollen,
a grain of silence

and
the well-guarded
honey
of prayer.

Văratec Monastery
July 23, 2001

Chimney Sweepers between Millenia

On earth, sweepers have little charm.
You have to watch them crucified above town
to really see them.
In the pub's vaulting, their voices barely flicker,
far from the white smoke bought with life's soot.

Here come the sweepers, lambs in arms,
solitude's acrobats
pirouetting
above us
in a town with no chimneys
in a time without lambs.

Poem in January

Snow left us,
its cover
so perfect.

Nobody composes any more
sonatas for the moon.
Not even sonatinas
for the confident smile
of infatuated teens.

It's dusking inside and outside
and I'm trying to imagine
the radiant sleep
of bees,
or the candles' wax
dripping melodiously
over so many prayers.

The lighthouse keeper
is baking apples, for sure.
Now she sits at the window
to be the first to see the wind's shadow.
At night, after she recites her prayer,
between the precise signals of the beacon,
she lets slip the same words:
"To fall like a man, to ascend like an angel!"

Luggage

She packs her luggage:
dresses and more dresses,
blouses and blouses,
books and more books,
necklaces and earrings and pins.
Then she remembers
the habits of the monk Nicodemus:
all rags,
their blackness washed out by sun and rain.
The mind fills
with the green echo
resonating from Isaac's words:
"The monastic habit, my son,
you will wear only
after you hang it outside
for three days
and nobody steals it."

Spring Fire

Equinox, 1999

I raked all day
my little garden,
gathered what's redundant
to this timid spring.

Then built a small fire
out of dried raspberry
and rose branches.
What scents suddenly rose
above life's grays!
"Clean place," mother would have said,
"Festive place,"
but where have my holy days gone?

I can't gather
either in my soul
or in the souls around me
all the dross,
can't destroy
what doesn't resemble love.
So I keep
raking conscientiously
my little earthly garden
with my daily prayer.

The Barn

To Adriana and Ilie

"Your house, your fortress," he would say, the grandfather from Apold,
the village gathered between vineyard-clad hills
like clear water in the hollow of a child's hand.

I'd push open the heavy oaken gate,
enter with my wagon the yard layered with river stones
like a Roman foot soldier
in the new fortress
that he'll mark, at dusk,
on the calf-skin map,
christening it again.

Evenings smelled of burning wood,
cornmeal,
and milk collected in a clay pitcher.
Unearthly music
competed with crickets and grasshoppers.

Then the second fortress would open for me,
the dark and lofty barn
filled with minor mysteries:
hay blending with calves' warm breath,
shadows illuminated
by the coppery shine of horses
and tools resting dutifully—

rakes, shovels, hoes,
the stubborn plough
back on the wall in its place of honor
like a coat of arms,
the wooden saddle
and harness.

Then I would climb the ladder
that took me to the hay pen
where sleep was without doubt most regal
and stillness would borrow the scent of dusking fields.

This is what heaven must be like
after you've mounted Jacob's ladder.

Sibiu
July 14, 1999

Prayer

I'm hollow,
a walnut emptied by a crow.

I'm lonely,
a loose cobblestone.

I'm bones without flesh,
raw wound
that no silk robe
or even the whitest lilac bush
can dress.

An orphaned word,
I live in the valley of cacti.

If only God would adopt me.

Bucharest
May 4, 1999

Dusk with Poet

Night sleeps in the village darkened by rain
like a key
rusting on the floor of the sea.
Ravens no longer leave their nests,
and buttresses don't prop the poet's dream
of returning to the window above the stairway
in the tower that separates our two cities.

Now that night
lashes its dogs
and the sledge is buried under snow,
no one recognizes him.

Sibiu
May 5, 1999

The One Who Leaves Few Footprints in the Snow

To Thomas Merton

He splits wood,
leaves few footprints in the snow—
their life shorter than that of the small
pine tree fire
above which he warms his hands
before dovetailing
the icon frames—
before taking back to his hut an ice cube,
water he'll use at twilight
to make coffee,
its black eye—sole indulgence,
its fragrant eye—sole gratification.

He leaves few footprints in the snow
and they're quickly erased by birds
for whom he sows wheat and crumbs
under the window where he reads the Psalms.

Kentucky, Abbey of Gethsemani
January 21, 2000

Poem with Wicket in Stephen the Great's Bell Tower

To Gheorghe Lazăr din Şuşag

To fall asleep with your head
on a bed of wild strawberries,
the sky above—
an incensed prayer.

The hermit's body—thurible
amid his brothers, the pine trees.

In the bell tower,
Lazarus of Şuşag, the Barefoot,
illuminates the ice between his fingers.
In his hand, the candle
lights itself.

The Light of the Psalms

How soothing the recollection of Mother Evghenia
conversing with blue flowers
in her hut—honeycomb beaming
from the hills of Văratec.

"Nameless flowers, like orphans.
I kept them warm,
they wintered under my bed."

"Had enough light?"
I asked, incredulous.

"They had light.
Plenty of light
as thick as honey
and airy as the star
in the Maiden's tears,
and pleasant to inhale
like the raspberry pyre
that girdles the fir woods,
and wasn't I reading, day and night,
right above them, the Psalms?"

Văratec Monastery
July 20, 2001

Poem with Stairway to the Hermit's Hut

To be one name concealing another
as the sheep's shadow brushes the cranberry bush

To be a stairway concealing another
as a prayer veils a child's mouth

To be a word covering silence
like a sunray over a river's source

To be a cave covering a name
like St. Jerome's hand stroking the lion's mane

Father Cleopa

What connection could there be
between the moss-covered door of the monk
and this daylight filling my room with TV
and thick carpets?
Where does communication between us
quicken or break?
His words speak even when unuttered,
echo through the forest, sweeten the air
that presages pending snows:
"Heaven take you," they say,
and the echo brings back the distant *toaca*:
"Patience, patience, patience…"

A thread of smoke rises
from the forest's mound of leaves
like the smile
of the one who, after reaching toward the Cross,
descends toward us.

Through the darkness slashed by wild strawberry pyres
saunters the angel hugging the moss-covered door in both arms.

Stigmata

After Giotto's angels,
and after His open wounds—
hot tears hung on cold stars—
sprung back to life in the beggar's palm,
after the eyes fixing you from the hospital bed,
how can you go on living
in oblivion?

You struggle with despair
and joy too
as you unearth
the words long-forgotten
under the tongue of memory
as if from a well
from which your bucket scoops
fish and gentians and sun
and the water's eye is neither troubled
nor startled.

Our childhood game: "One star for you, one for me,"
you'd like to play again
this late December night
when others
beckon
the Magi back
from oblivion.

First Day at Văratec Monastery

The nun's voice sketches
a small, cypress cross
when she recites the Psalms.

A little girl steps through the gate,
and joyful, shy, and flustered, attempts
the sign of the cross.
Her tiny fingers gather
the Holy Trinity
with innocent reverence.

A nun gifts me with flowers from her garden—
three white,
three blue.
"Don't cut any more for me, a sinner," I tell her.

"I need another color," she returns.
"Three flowers, just like the Trinity.
And three colors. The third, the color of your spirit."

If I Lift My Eyes

From where I lie in bed,
I watch a dirt road winged with poplar trees,
recent summers' "royal path"
connecting one village to one monastery.
And there're also the roadside white poppies
brushing Sister Evlampia's dark habits
near the sluice where children love to play,
near the house of the recluse who cultivates only stars
in his little garden on the slope along the river.

It's summer up there,
no, autumn,
for I see grape pickers
hanging perfectly from this last thread of light
that threatens to descend upon my poem and die,
so I stop writing
lest I lose it.

From where I lie in bed
in this American room,
if only I lift my eyes
I see the monastery in vespers light
and young Sister Agripina
whose palms still bear
the imprint
of the knell's rope.

Messenger

Whose and what kind of messenger
are you, small bird,
forever melted in the walnut's bark?
Your blue neckband alone
does not dissolve
in the embers in which
I've dressed my life.

A tiny window
in the sweltering, lunar trunk
flaunts a prayer book.
How well you halt against His light
and how you sweep the ashes off my path
till you restore its melody,
its blue.

At times I'm a scythe in a lonely woman's hands,
other times the wild strawberry
on the mountain path.

Poem Composed while Being Watched by a Bird

To Dana

Let your soles touch the grass
gracefully, as in childhood,
when you swam among stars.

Let your step be soundless,
and wordless your glance.
To hush your headaches,
bare your feet and tread the grass
as if learning your first words
on mother's lap.

May the leaves' rust never descend upon your soul.
May twilight draw rich flowers
on your eyelids
while angels' lips
teach you once more
how to pray.

Bucharest
September 3, 2000

In the Heart of the Forest

To be in the heart of the forest
and talk money
—like plucking feathers off a bird
ready to stuff it
while listening
to Bach, Mozart, Palestrina.

Braşov
August 2, 2012

Poem with Blueberries, Fog, and Sibiu

"A quois bon quitter Coasta Boacii?" —Emil Cioran

I walk slowly down Balului Street
with a blueberry basket and a book.
"*L'inverno: maestoso…*" Vivaldi whispers
from his house with owls in the windows.

Today my hands smell of fog, fir, and night
because they touched a meteor;
that's why I wear rings
and, in my hair, the tinsel of the last comet.

A young man walks by, stooping under the weight of his blueberry basket—
poems spill out of his pockets,
and he tells me with sadness as we reach the village at dawn:
"I can't read a poem by Nichita Stănescu
just anywhere, in any mood, Miss,
for it's not a recipe,
but an utterance, a fir tree needling the heavens."

When the "snow eater" blows from Cindrel,
I dream of blueberries, summer, and my hoard of crystalline words.

Knees blushing with clearings' wild strawberries,
I come down thinking of the fern that breathes
only in shade, in the forest of kept secrets,
away from drums and brass bands.

I follow the meandering path
like an ivory rain in the night.

My basket spills over the world
and a shadow appears:
Cioran, his lips stained by the last blueberries,

writing on air, under the timid light corseting the mountain:
"The ratio between joy and sorrow
approaches harmony."

History of a Couple

The bluish call of peacocks
deep into the Sibiu night,
the sun wrapped in snoring,
the rueful tunes of a saxophone
—and a drum much like an ice cube clinking
against the crystal glass—
while the cold shadows of singers
sink deeper and deeper into snow
and a furious tiger
pulls apart my dreaming flesh.

The Tower of Steps

You bridge the town below with the town above.
Your steps are made of spears
that pierce the spines of some stars, true,
but mostly the spines of dragons.

At the bottom, a golden barrel
stuffed with comets, words,
and tears, mostly tears.

The green eye of the moss
lights your way
and silence alone is your fortress.

Whoever enters through your narrow door
will walk the green path forever.

Someone pulls the curtains
on the tower of Sibiu
and I'm facing the tower of Manhattan
where the poet returns each winter
to unspool memories of a feverish childhood.
The only stairs in the stairless hotel:
a crucifix.

Landscape with Poet

How you sleep in the white clock tower—
a bee, one might think, its wings caught in the golden
pinions of the tall lily.
Your shadow measures the lives below
on the tarmac swarming with children who grow old as they play.
Or the life of the woman guarding the rifles of past centuries' soldiers;
the beam glides on her face like a gecko
(when some visitor bothers to climb the tower)
and her hands, large and absent,
lost in the black of her black skirt,
suddenly take flight.
Soon the snows will arrive.

Painting with Late Night in Păltiniş

Late at night, school day,
in the kitchen,
under the lamp's halo,
father repairing a small pair of skis.

In the window: the mountain.
A doll in my arms
and the roof of my mouth inked with first words.

On the radio: Vivaldi.

Louisville
January 25, 2001

Harmonia Mundi

At the border between garden and orchard,
an old door
with a rusted padlock. Rusted by rain or dew?

We walk through it barefoot, blissful, cherubic.
My name: Volatile.

Grandmother's apron, a white cloud
scented with lavender
under which I'd bend my head
when the lamb gave birth,
sowing the air with as many photons
as star seeds
over hills, in summertime.

Then, the timeless joy—
children by the pond
gazing at the orange mill
brimming with moon.

Under the beam,
the braid of garlic cloves
—tiny lanterns
illuminating my height
on the spine of the door,
marked there by father,

his hands fragranced with walnuts,
and on the windowsill
the little sack of seeds waiting to defrost.

At the border between clay and star,
a narrow door
through which only we, children,
could squeeze,
on a path of light.

Bucharest
December 16, 2005

The Main Square

The insomniac gaze
of the houses crammed
into each other
like birds
in nests
the night
before
journeying
toward warm shores.

The Little Square

Needlework
stitched by an angel
on the winter
solstice night.

Between the Wheat Wells and the Bridal Mirrors

In the main square, where ropemakers sell rope
and shoemakers shoes,
the shadow of the three moons floating evenings above town
is caught in the butterfly net of children,

while furrier Brid fills his well with wheat.
The same happens in the Little Square
where Nicolaus the goldsmith places the clean fruit of his work
in the cabinet under the three moons floating evenings
above town.

Who will spark the blades and kitchen knives
now that the sharpener's house has been demolished
and Sibiu shimmers with June bugs?

Luckily, the poet has a working room for bridal mirrors
and a net for catching beautiful dreams
not too far from the Bark Mill.
Each night, down in the Golden Valley, he flies kites made of poems
penned with his friend, J. G. Bayer, hatmaker and illustrious orator.

The Tower of Welders

Towers behind me
in the photo you took before we left for the New World.

Welders rise from the Old World
like the dry wine of Apold rises
from the tower's cellars.
They smell of young wood as they sit there,
next to cannonballs, savoring bread with smoked lard,
ready to defend Sibiu.

The fortress is somewhere behind,
the defense trench
now an ordinary park
with green flanks on which high school kids kiss
and retirees read the paper unperturbed.

Its stone body, pierced by a single beam as by a tunnel
—the Sentry Path
propped now by wide, serene arches
as well as bleeding molds of day and night.

We threw cherries
through its tiny windows,
called each other's names
with palms cupped into funnels, happy.

How words ran
between our soft, incandescent fingers.
As if they belonged to angels.

The Street of Measuring Scales

In the town below the mountain,
a street through which a bridge
rushes.
On the corner facing the world,
a pub, "To the Holed Fluffy Coat."
Opposite, a small house
filled with drawers
from which an old woman
digs out all kinds of candies
for neighborhood kids.

A giant walnut tree in the middle of the street
shelters my grandparents' house,
also a well and a pear tree so wild
winter nights
it whinnied,
and when it died
we tied our sleighs to it.

Mother told stories about picking golden pears,
about Zeppelin steering his airship
above our town,
about her first waltz with our father
at "The Roman Emperor,"
and how the government ordered
"streets be lit only on nights without moon."

One snowstorm night, she
pulled out of an old glove
a silver coin passed down father to son,
a coin whose fading letters read,
"God, take pity on us all."

The Bridge over the Train Station

The garden was always blue
and the house in which grandmother read Ibsen lay under the walnut tree,
at the crossroads.
The well mixed its crisp, clean scent
with the whistling of the train,
the polished buffer beams of the locomotive
about which grandfather bragged while shaving
in an old crystal mirror carried through snowstorms
all the way from Vienna
by the artist in our family.

In the kitchen that smelled of boiled potatoes
and baked apples,
of quiet life and bustling children
who bit into words as into gigantic slices of dark bread
topped with apricot jam,

I was praying to my angel,
wishing for a rainless Sunday
so I could go to the grove and feed the fish
and for mother to buy me a ring with a red stone
and a pram for my rag doll
which had not even a name.
Why would things need a name
when they are so visible, so loved?

Now, an old child,
I still dream the bridge over the train station,
those trains passing through my lacquered shoes
at dream speed, dizzy from watching
words
cut the air
while heading for foreign countries.
Or the triumphant cry of sailors on the brink of sinking,
navigare est necesse, vivere non est necesse...

Bucharest
November 20, 2000

In the Burgh of Yesteryear

In the burgh of yesteryear my brother tamed Sundays
and when he could no more, no more, he'd scratch off
with his nails the shadows he threw on walls.
In the burgh of yesteryear I was both the clocksmith
and the one who placed the heavy iron arm
on the frail hour of the tower.
You'd pick wild strawberries on the lip of the precipice.
One word and we both tumbled in.

Healings

I drink milk late at night, in the mountains.
Its lonesome white
a beam
that carries
the melting snow
of mother's breast—

a moment of healing
for the child
I continue to be
and for whom
you return from death, always,

mother.

Shards of Happiness

St. Seren the gardener harvests stars from gardens,
places them on pantry shelves, in the company of apples,

then feeds them prayers
till they ascend back to the heavens.

Vila Dobruşa
June, 2011

Mother's Birth Year

I search through the chronicles of our city
for my mother's birth year.
By the side of the Ursulines Monastery
I leaf through them,
year by year,
sunrise by sunrise,
sunset by sunset,
and discover, among other things,
that the king himself attended
that year's unveiling of a monument
honoring the officers
lost to the First World War.
Oh, Europe, little square
crowded with statues
turned, so often, into shooting targets,
with people drowning in sadness.

But let me return to the year of grace 1926:
The queen,
choked with emotion and long strings of pearls,
attended the horse races
of the School of Cavalry Officers.
Between these events,
on July 14, a cloud broke loose.

In my grandparents' yard, on Scales Street no.10,
the plates of the scale must have remained perfectly balanced:
One held the harmony of the house,
the other the tender smile of little Elena.

Sitting at the Table with My Angel in Patmos

Father, I sit at the table with my angel,
telling him about you:
how at seventy you planted a hundred fruit trees
and about the diary tallying your spring labor,
your autumn labor,
and about your book on train engines,
but especially about your love for mother,
how it still breathes in the letters
I found wrapped in her bridal veil,
and how you painted all my doors white.
"Doors open on their own to good people,"
you told me, smiling,
"and your steps, my child, will open paths
to clean places, unbeknownst to you yet,"

and my guardian angel whispered,
"Become a peddler of worthy things."

Years have passed, father,
and I'm on this holy island
talking with my angel
about your big heart,
how it cradled us
while you doled out large slices of peace.

In the cave of the Apocalypse
I prayed, with my angel,

to St. John the Evangelist,
the disciple who rested his head on God's chest
just as I rested mine so many times on yours, father,
shield for my interior storms
while I prayed arduously to my angel
to look after us,
I, still on Earth,
you already in heaven.

Skala, Patmos
June 6, 2010

Sibiu Rain

Raining in Sibiu, white, grey, black—the sky
an impenetrable safebox.
Leaning against our fence,
bride's flowers,
also called "coins of mercy."
On the street, the fanfare
accompanying a wedding or funeral procession.

Strange, these monotonous rains—
sometimes grey, sometimes white, even black at times,
something sad and cheap about them,
like the Parisian theatres of the '30s
screening films enhanced, on stage, with piano music,
or like a dog's stiff body
in dew-covered grass.

Even now I startle awake at midnight
with rain streaming down my shoulders,
and Johann playing the trumpet with such anguish, up in the cold attic,
next to his father's hanging body.

The Windows of Visby

So many decorate their windows:
sailboats, schooners, ships,
even train engines,
horses and lighthouses
—idyllic encapsulations of the idea of journey

    and
everyone, absolutely everyone,
even those who adorn them
with fans, scales, tiny ballerinas,
eggs, candlesticks, lonely lamps
and birds, especially birds

hides a dream,
always the same one
    and
they hide it deftly
in the hem of a skirt
or the lining of an overcoat:

run, quick, run.

Visby
June 7, 2009

The Room on the Island

The room on the island
windows perfectly round
music sheets for walls

the lamp
a giant white swan.

For Jean Weigl

Sometimes the angel descends
in a little white car.
She has dark long hair and eyes even darker.
She has two children: a boy and an adopted daughter.
She runs back and forth between the skating rink
the size of a frozen tear
on which the soul dares risky pirouettes
and the art studio
where Bruce draws angels
who keep getting older and older.

Last night,
burdened as only angels can be,
electrical pillows in place of wings,
she descended with the thermal blanket and a steamy bag of apples
to put rocks on my feet
and warm, with her wings,
my cold American room.
We talked about our children,
our men,
but mostly about God,
about what you could possibly offer
a black-haired
wide-eyed, black-eyed
angel

if not another angel:
small, bluish,
painted by Giotto in Padova
only two days ago,
while deep in sadness—

State College, PA
November 2, 1997

And Here Goes Tess, on Nygatan Street

And here goes Tess, tresses like flames,
on a white bicycle
on Nygatan Street.
She rides in from the Baltic Sea,
from afar,
all the way from Port Angeles.

She rides in humming an old Irish song,

a blackbird on her shoulder,
on the other a nest

and once she reaches the shore
she starts spinning stories
about how beautiful the world,
so beautiful she makes us see it
through the eyes of a colt.

Visby, Gotland
June, 2009

Matache Market Seen from Boston

In the tiny gardens on Commonwealth Avenue
some crocuses and daffodils sprout next to snow piles,
and so does the strutting blue-purple cabbage
treated here, in America, as ornamental plant
resembling a young ballerina
sheathed in translucent tulle.

How distant she keeps herself from her sister in the Matache Market:
greenish pale, perfect for the poor's favorite dishes
or for pickling over winter.

"Sour cabbage, wide-leafed, sour cabbage
for *sarmale*," calls out the auntie from Bucovina,
queen of barrels brimming with pickled cabbage.

Saturday with Blizzard and the Council Tower

Saturday blizzard in Cişmigiu
and the beggar's feeding pigeons.
Some eat directly from his palm
like the bear from St. Seraphim's hand
in the desolate forest.

Few are the passersby who stop
and even fewer who listen.
He has a word or two for each
—seeds for frozen souls.

"Your home lodges a deaf thing, the past,"
he smiles, kindly,
then lifts both arms in the frozen air.
The pigeons take off
happy, unfazed
by the briskness of his gesture.

Saturday with the blizzards of 2005.
After three centuries and three weeks,
the tiny grey bird with all-orange chest
returns to my window.
"Mandarina," I name her.

Once upon a time, she was the Council Town of Sibiu,
first defense tower, then grain silo,
fire tower,
prison,
and finally science museum.

Bored with the bustle
and with the clock's deafening strokes,
she traded her body of stone
for that of a tiny
grey bird,
its chest solid orange.

Silent Tongue

The light in the eyes
of the omniscient doe
braver than ever
when readying
to leap over the precipice.

The Biblical Garden of San Francisco

I live in this Bucharest February
as if stranded on an iceberg.

Could this be a tower, a lighthouse?
Or a long-coming punishment?

Only a year ago,
I lived in an oceanic February.
My feet drifted
to the Biblical Gardens
of San Francisco.
I strolled along paths
laced with magnolia and camellia.
Poppies white and red and hoary
glistened amid rocks
like the tears of myrrh-bearing women.
Waves of lavender cooled off
my exhausted ankles,
and as I passed under its royal wreath
myrrh spurs kissed my forehead as in a dream.

Anemone, sage, and rosemary
whispered their psalms.
On open palms, daffodils ferried me
over the ocean
to my departed father's garden,

home,
to mountain paths
guarded by strawberries and translucent crocuses
and marked by a roadside crucifix
inscribed with the words of the old anchorite:
"Come here, you devil, it's confession time."

The Child Speaks

Tears down his cheeks
then onto the paper meant to capture spring.
When asked about his parents, he blurts:
"At night mother washes the stars
and during the day clothes for two families.
Evenings she irons out words, to unwrinkle them.

And father,
father puts lipsticks on fish
at the market
so they're always fresh."

Flight Lesson at the Baltic Sea

Yesterday I took flight lessons
with a seagull,
and dance lessons too.

Half bird, half human,
I felt
these arms flexed for flight
but also for dance
these arms
that keep me balanced
on the daily tightrope.

Visby
June 19, 2009

Words as Gladiolas

To dig words out of silence
    the way father
    dug up gladiola bulbs
    so tenderly
—my stars, he'd whisper
    while arranging their sleeping bodies
    in crates lined with white paper
    or the pages of old cookie recipes.

Andantino

Like dandelion seeds,
an angel's underwing,
the skin inside a lamb's ear
—the words
to comfort your kin.

Notes

"Father Cleopa": *Toaca* is a board made generally of wood, but sometimes of iron, curved if fixed between supports and straight when meant to be carried. The rhythmical patterns created by the beats of a small mallet against the board call the faithful to prayer. Monk Cleopa (1912-1998) resisted the initial pressures of the communist regime by living, in the late '40s and '50s, as a hermit in Romania's forests. After his return to the monastery of Sihăstria, his reputation as a learned holy man spread, and for the next decades steady streams of pilgrims came to hear his teachings.

"Matache Market": *Sarmale* are pickled cabbage leaves stuffed with meat, rice, and spices.

Born in Sibiu, Romania, **Liliana Ursu** has published ten books of poetry in Romanian, most recently the selected *Loc Ferit/ Haven*. Her first book in English, *The Sky Behind the Forest* (Bloodaxe Books, 1997), translated by Adam J. Sorkin and Tess Gallagher with the poet, was shortlisted for Oxford's Weidenfeld Prize, and *Lightwall* (Zephyr, 2009), translated by Sean Cotter, was a finalist for the PEN USA 2010 Literary Award in Translation. Ursu, who has been awarded Romania's rank of Knight of Arts and Literature, is also the recipient of two Fulbright grants and has taught creative writing at the University of Louisville and at Bucknell University.

Mihaela Moscaliuc is the author of *Immigrant Model* (University of Pittsburgh Press, 2015) and *Father Dirt* (Alice James Books, 2010), translator of Carmelia Leonte's *The Hiss of the Viper* (Carnegie Mellon University Press, 2015), and editor of *Insane Devotion: On the Writing of Gerald Stern* (Trinity University Press, 2016). A former Fulbright Scholar, Moscaliuc is associate professor of English at Monmouth University and visiting faculty in the Drew University MFA Program in Poetry and Poetry in Translation.

Books by Liliana Ursu

Poetry in Romanian:

Viața deasupra orașului (Cartea Românească, 1977)

Ordinea clipelor (Cartea Românească, 1978)

Piața aurarilor (Cartea Românească, 1980)

Zona de protecție (Eminescu, 1983)

Corali (Eminescu, 1986)

Înger călare pe fiară (Cartea Românească, 1996)

Sus să avem inimile (Eminescu, 2001)

Cartea Farurilor/Book of Lighthouses. Bilingual edition, translated by
   Bruce Weigl and the author (Pontica, 2003)

Gradina din Turn—Der Garten im Turm. Bilingual edition (Info-Art
        Media, 2012)
Loc Ferit, poeme alese. Bilingual edition (Baroque Books and Arts, 2014)

PROSE IN ROMANIAN:
La jumătatea drumului (Cartea Românească, 1986)
Visul (Glasul, 1985)

TRANSLATIONS BY URSU FROM ENGLISH/ROMANIAN INTO ROMANIAN/ENGLISH:
Polenul Insidios/Deceptive Pollen, by Martin Booth, translated with Dinu
        Flămând (Univers, 1977)
Norii Magdalenici/The Magellanic Clouds by Diane Wakoski (Univers,
        1978)
15 Young Romanian Poets (Eminescu, 1982)
*Trei poeţi britanici contemporani/Three contemporary British poets: Fleur
        Adcock, Alan Brownjohn, Jon Silkin*, translated with Denisa
        Comănescu and Mircea Ivănescu (Univers, 1989)
Fires on Water, Seven Poets from Sibiu, translated with Adam J. Sorkin,
        (Cartea Românească, 1992)
Dinner at the Table of Silence, Writers from Gorj, translated with Sean
        Cotter (Vlusium, 2002)
Taci, te rog!/ Will You Please Be Quiet, Please? by Raymond Carver
        (Polirom, 2004)
Treasury of the City / Vistieriile cetatii, 18 Poets of Sibiu (Institutul
        Cultural Român, 2008)

POETRY TRANSLATED INTO ENGLISH:
The Sky Behind the Forest, translated by Liliana Ursu, Adam J. Sorkin,
        and Tess Gallagher (Bloodaxe Books, 1997)
Angel Riding a Beast, translated by Bruce Weigl and Liliana Ursu
        (Northwestern UP, 1998)

Goldsmith Market, translated by Sean Cotter (Zephyr Press, 2003)
Lightwall, translated by Sean Cotter (Zephyr Press, 2009)
A Path to the Sea, translated by Liliana Ursu, Adam J. Sorkin, and Tess
  Gallagher (Pleasure Boat Studio, 2011)

Books from Etruscan Press

Etruscan Press Is Proud of Support Received From

Wilkes University

Youngstown State University

The Ohio Arts Council

The Stephen & Jeryl Oristaglio Foundation

The Nathalie & James Andrews Foundation

The National Endowment for the Arts

The New Mexico Community Foundation

Founded in 2001 with a generous grant from the Oristaglio Foundation, Etruscan Press is a nonprofit cooperative of poets and writers working to produce and promote books that nurture the dialogue among genres, achieve a distinctive voice, and reshape the literary and cultural histories of which we are a part.

etruscan press
www.etruscanpress.org
Etruscan Press books may be ordered from

Consortium Book Sales and Distribution
800.283.3572
www.cbsd.com

Etruscan Press is a 501(c)(3) nonprofit organization.
Contributions to Etruscan Press are tax deductible
as allowed under applicable law.
For more information, a prospectus,
or to order one of our titles,
contact us at books@etruscanpress.org.